CH01023660

Flying Scots
A Celebration in Stamps
the preservation of 4472 told
by stamps, covers and postcards

By Alan Rigby

I acknowledge with thanks the support and permission given to me by the following companies in order to use facsimiles of their Souvenir covers. Thanks are also due to the companies no longer in business who produced Flying Scotsman souvenir covers in the past. Buckingham Covers, Folkestone Kent CT19 4BF

BFDC Ltd, 3 Link Road, Stoneygate, Leicester, LE2 3RA, United Kingdom.

The Benham Group, Folkestone, Kent, CT19 4RG.

ISBN 978-0-9935795-1-6

All profits from this publication will be donated to the National Railway Museum and the railway preservation movement to help with preservation of steam locomotives and in particular Flying Scotsman

DEDICATIONS

To my wife Pat for her patience and understanding of life with a steam enthusiast /stamp collector

Also to Alan Pegler, Sir William McAlpine, Pete Waterman and Tony Marchington whose dedication, enthusiasm and finances together with the willingness and time of countless volunteers and supporters kept Flying Scotsman on the rails, culminating in the success of the appeal to buy it for the nation.

SUMMARY OF CONTENTS

The attempt I have made, in producing this book, is to list and illustrate the time in preservation of Flying Scotsman by showing, in chronological order, the stamps, cards and covers in my collection in the following sections :-

Celebrating the legend of Flying Scotsman with stamps, covers, postcards and philatelic ephemera

An illustrated philatelic story of the time spent in heritage preservation by the Flying Scotsman since1963, using my collection of related stamps, souvenir covers, postcards, photographs, ephemera and memorabilia to tell the story. Addresses have been removed for privacy reasons. A lifelong love of steam locomotives and of stamp collecting has led to this story.

In the late 1970s Flying Scotsman was stabled at Steam Town in Carnforth in Lancashire where we had a caravan. In addition to visiting 4472 in the sheds we were able to travel behind her and Sir Nigel Gresley on the Cumbrian Coast line to Ravenglass where the added steam attraction was Little Ratty, the Ravenglass and Eskdale Railway, but that is another story. These experiences however led to a love of 4472 Flying Scotsman and the philatelic collection that I share here.

Two of our family photographs from a journey behind 4472 to Ravenglass in 1979. My family can be seen to the left of the left hand photograph. Below is a Ravenglass and Eskdale railway cover cover from 1979 showing 4472 on the railway stamp .

The nations favourite locomotive was built at Doncaster in 1923 as an A1 4/6/2 Pacific for use on the Train of the same name from Kings Cross to Edinburgh, on the east coast main line. It's path to fame as the nations favourite locomotive was instigated when it was chosen to be an exhibit at the 1924 British Exhibition . Below are two souvenir covers that celebrate the 80th anniversary of the British Empire Exhibition 1924 and depict the Flying Scotsman.

Flying Scotsman was always a favourite amongst steam locomotive enthusiasts (train spotters) in the days when it was just one of the locomotives rostered to haul the train of the same name from Kings Cross to Edinburgh every day. However from 1963 in the private ownership of Alan Pegler, who bought it from British Rail for £3000, it gradually became the worlds best known and favourite steam locomotive due to the tours it made both at home and abroad.

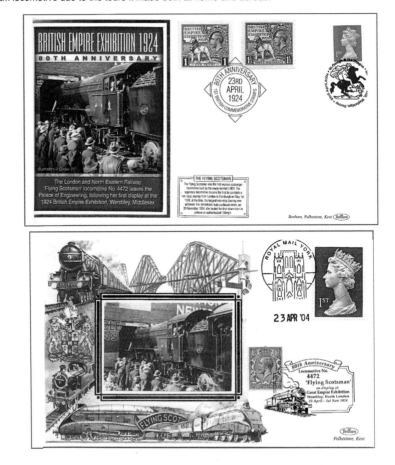

Flying Scotsman was displayed at the Great Empire Exhibition in 1924 in LNER lime green livery and carrying No. 4472. The locomotive was displayed at Wembley, North London from April 23rd until November 1st 1924, representing the latest in locomotive design. She was a huge success and returned to the exhibition in 1925. Built in Doncaster, she was named after the famous express train in 1923.

Alongside is a facsimile of the LNER brochure for the exhibition that includes detailed engineering drawings of the locomotive including the full side elevation and plan of the locomotive also shown below.

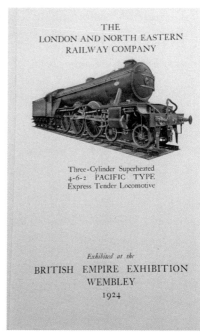

THE
LONDON AND NORTH EASTERN
RAILWAY COMPANY

Three-Cylinder Superheated
4-6-2 PACIFIC TYPE
Express Tender Locomotive

Exhibited at the
BRITISH EMPIRE EXHIBITION
WEMBLEY
1924

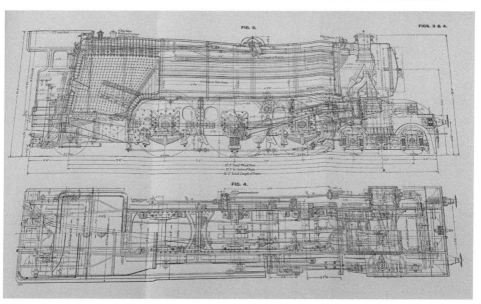

The following illustrations of post cards issued by the Dalkeith postcard company illustrate the building of the Flying Scotsman and its early use.

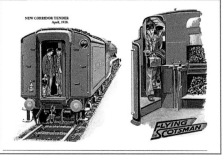

LONDON AND NORTH EASTERN RAILWAY
CLASS A1 No. 4472 "FLYING SCOTSMAN". DESIGNED BY SIR NIGEL GRESLEY

In the following years postcards were issued and illustrate Flying Scotsman in its different early

LNER liveries and operating with the double tender.

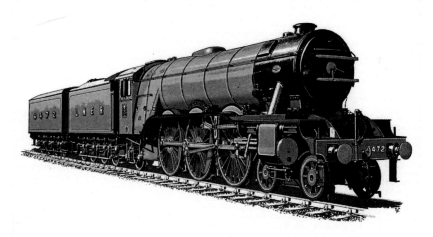

LONDON AND NORTH EASTERN RAILWAY
CLASS A3 No. 4472 "FLYING SCOTSMAN". DESIGNED BY SIR NIGEL GRESLEY

These two Postcards published by Valentines show the superb side views of the 4.6.2 Pacific

Flying Scotsman as an A1 and also a similar view of its predecessor Great Northern the first 4.6.2

built by the Great Northern Railway prior to the formation of the LNER. The cards also give the

specifications of the locomotives.

"FLYING SCOTSMAN," L.N.E.R., 4472. 4-6-2. 3-CYLINDER ENGINE. TYPE A.1.

ONE OF THE WORLD'S MOST POPULAR ENGINES, AND USED FOR THE FAMOUS LONDON TO ABERDEEN RUN.

GAUGE OF TRACK	4 FT. 8½ INS.	FIRE BOX WIDTH	7 FT. 9 INS.
CYLINDERS	20 INS. x 26 INS.	TUBES	NUMBER 168, DIAMETER 2¼ INS.
DRIVING WHEEL DIAMETER	6 FT. 8 INS.		32 „ 5¼ INS.
BOILER INSIDE DIAMETER	6 FT. 3 5/8 INS.	8-WHEELED CORRIDOR TENDER.	
PRESSURE	180 LBS.	CAPACITY WATER	5000 GALLONS
FIRE BOX LENGTH	9 FT. 5¼ INS.	COAL	9 TONS

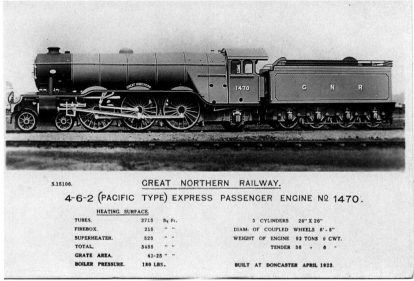

S.15106.

GREAT NORTHERN RAILWAY.

4-6-2 (PACIFIC TYPE) EXPRESS PASSENGER ENGINE N⁰ 1470.

HEATING SURFACE.			
TUBES,	2715 Sq Ft.	3 CYLINDERS 20" X 26"	
FIREBOX.	215 " "	DIAM. OF COUPLED WHEELS 6'-8"	
SUPERHEATER.	525 " "	WEIGHT OF ENGINE 92 TONS 9 CWT.	
TOTAL,	3455 " "	TENDER 56 " 6 "	
GRATE AREA.	41·25 " "		
BOILER PRESSURE.	180 LBS.	BUILT AT DONCASTER APRIL 1922.	

The Flying Scotsman.

The Train.

The post card alongside illustrates the Flying Scotsman timetable starting at 10 am from both ends in the early 1950s. Many of the LNER posters, related to the Flying Scotsman, have been reproduced as postcards. Some from my collection are reproduced here.

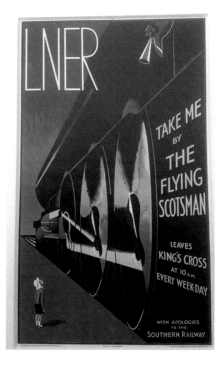

The two postcards below were used and carried on the steam hauled Flying Scotsman on 4th October 1997 hauled by 60007 Sir Nigel Gresley and signed by other passengers and staff.

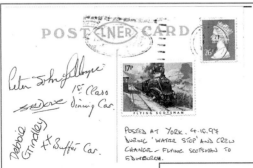

There have been many souvenir covers produced related to the Flying Scotsman train and its achievements, many featuring the famous trains set of stamps issued in 1985, illustrated by Terence Cuneo the railway artist, some of which are reproduced below. The first being a first day cover of the complete set. We however only interested in the Flying Scotsman stamp illustrating our famous train hauled by an A4 and signed by the designer Terence Cuneo.

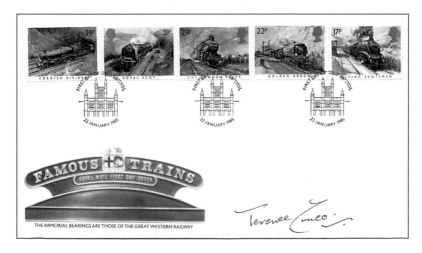

The cover below is again of the complete set but on a cover from Steamtown in Carnforth where my story started and includes an image of 4472.

Below are several examples of the use of the single stamp

The first example (top left) is the FlyingScotsman stamp used on a a maximum card, where the Royal Mail PHQ card is used with matching stamp and cancellation. (Top Right) is a post card and matching stamp used as a souvenir of the opening of the Durham philatelic counter. Below them is a miniature souvenir sheet issued for visitors to the 1985 Stampex philatelic exhibition held in London. This sheet has been overprinted 'Specimen' and a matching stamp and Stampex cachet added.

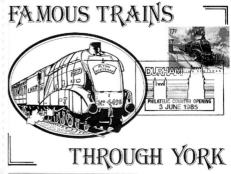

The final item in this section is a Postcard with a silk picture of Flying Scotsman issued at the at the same time as the famous train stamps but cancelled with a 150th anniversary of the Great Western Railway (GWR) postmark used at Kings Cross station.

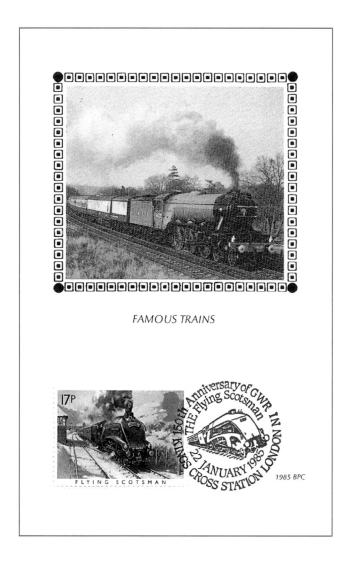

FAMOUS TRAINS

Flying Scotsman on stamps of other countries

Stamps featuring Flying Scotsman have been issued by several countries, many of whom do not have a railway and even less a claim to Flying Scotsman, but it just goes to show how famous the locomotive is throughout the world. Flying Scotsman is featured here on covers and miniature sheets as well as stamps. My personal favourite is shown first and is from St Lucia and is a se-tenant pair one stamp showing a view of Flying Scotsman and the other a technical drawing of the locomotive, and pictured with a first day of issue post mark.

Below are two of several types of the first day cover for the St . Lucia stamps that were part of the locomotives section of the Leaders of the World Series of sets of stamps.

In 1982 Grenada issued a very nice 90c value featuring Flying Scotsman that was presented on the card below, the reverse of which contained interesting facts about the locomotives history.

The reverse of the card is shown below.

FLYING SCOTSMAN

Throughout her long career, the London and North Eastern Railway engine known as the *Flying Scotsman* set many railway records . . . and was a pioneering force in the development and progress of the railroad throughout Europe. Each and every morning, for 121 years, the *Flying Scotsman* would leave Kings Cross at *exactly* 10:00 a.m. on her 292 mile trip to Edinburgh . . . the only British express which can claim such a remarkably reliable departure time. Early in her career, the *Flying Scotsman* could make her 292 mile express trip in 20½ hours. However, some one-hundred years later — and after several modifications — she would set new records by making the same trip in well under six hours. Aside from her remarkable increases in speed, this same locomotive is credited with regularly making the longest non-stop run in the world — her daily 292 mile express trip from Kings Cross to Edinburgh. During one particularly rainy year, many bridges were washed out by floods. To reach her destination, the *Flying Scotsman* took detours and increased her non-stop route to an incredible 408 miles . . . perhaps the longest non-stop express in the history of railroads. To accommodate the passengers and crew during these long, arduous trips, the *Flying Scotsman* was equipped with elegant dining cars and comfortable sleeping cars. Since this unique locomotive proved herself such an outstanding form of transportation, Grenada issued the stamp featured on this Display Card to honor the *Flying Scotsman*.

©1983 Fleetwood, Cheyenne, Wyoming, U.S.A. 71480A

Original painting by Basil Smith

A miniature sheet issued by Grenada of their trains of the world
set of stamps,including a one dollar Flying Scotsman stamp.

TRAINS OF THE WORLD

A block of 4 of a Lesotho Stamp featuring FlyingScotsman

A first day cover of the Lesotho Railways of the world set featuring the Flying Scotsman Stamp.

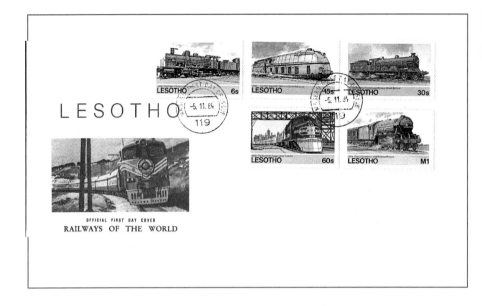

Even the Scottish Island of Staffa issued a local souvenir (Cinderella) stamp
for tourists that featured Flying Scotsman.

A miniature sheet issued by the Republic of Chad to celebrate the life of Sir Nigel Gresley. The sheet bears four super views of 4472 with and without smoke deflectors.

A miniature sheet issued by Liberia to celebrate great trains and Locomotives that includes the Flying Scotsman as 60103 in Brunswick green and carrying the German smoke deflectors.

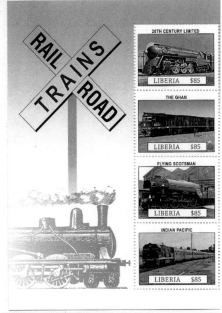

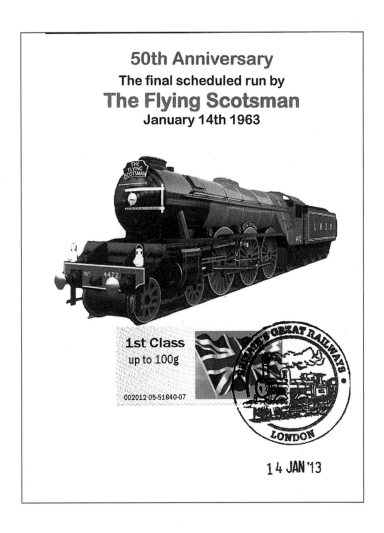

50th Anniversary
The final scheduled run by
The Flying Scotsman
January 14th 1963

A postcard issued to celebrate the 50th anniversary of the final scheduled run for Flying Scotsman on January 14th 1963. The card is franked with a ' post and go ' self adhesive stamp and cancelled with a Great British Trains cancel.

In 1962, British Railways announced that they would scrap Flying Scotsman. Number 60103 ended service with its last scheduled run on 14 January. It was proposed That it could be be saved by a group called "Save Our Scotsman", they were unable to raise the required £3,000, the scrap value of the locomotive.

Alan Pegler, who first saw the locomotive at the British Empire Exhibition in 1924, received £70,000 for his share holding when Northern Rubber was sold in 1961 to Pegler's Valves, a company started by his grandfather. When Flying Scotsman was due to be scrapped Alan Pegler stepped in and bought it outright, with the political support of Prime Minister Harold Wilson. He spent large amounts of money over the next few years having the locomotive restored at Doncaster Works as closely as possible to its LNER condition. The smoke deflectors were removed; the double chimney was replaced by a single chimney; and the tender was replaced by one of the corridor type with which the locomotive had run between 1928 and 1936. It was also repainted in LNER livery. Alan Pegler then persuaded the British Railways Board to let him run enthusiasts' specials, it was at the time the only steam locomotive running on mainline British Railways. It worked a number of rail tours, including a non-stop London–Edinburgh run in 1968, the year steam traction officially ended on BR. In the meantime, watering facilities for steam locomotives were disappearing, so in September 1966 Alan Pegler purchased a second corridor tender which was adapted as an auxiliary water tank but retaining its through gangway, this was coupled behind the normal tender.

LONDON AND NORTH EASTERN RAILWAY
CLASS A3 No. 4472 "FLYING SCOTSMAN". DESIGNED BY SIR NIGEL GRESLEY

I have found very little philatelic evidence for the Alan Pegler years until plans started for the U.S.A. Tour.

Alan Pegler had a contract permitting him to run his locomotive on British Rail until 1972.

The covers below, were issued for the Moorlands Rail Tour, hauled by Flying Scotsman,that was the last scheduled steam train to run on BR on 26/10/1968

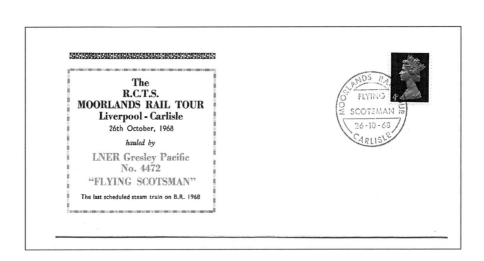

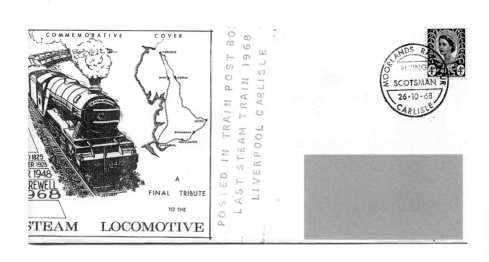

The following covers are souvenirs of the 1969 Flying Scotsman hauled, L.N.E.R. Summer Tour from London to York and return. There were lots of visits and tours over the 10 years of Alan Peglar's ownership but there doesn't seem to be many philatelic souvenirs produced, if there were they are well tucked away in collections. The first cover below bears a FLYING SCOTSMAN USA LTD label that appeared on the covers posted in the various destinations in the U.S.A

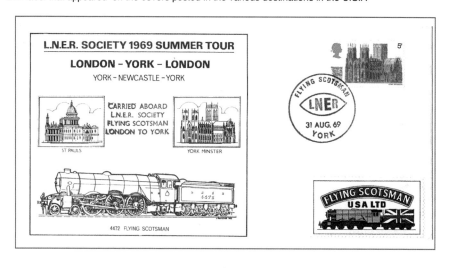

THE U.S.A TOUR.

Flying Scotsman was loaded aboard the SS Saxonia at Brocklebank dock in Liverpool for the 10 day journey to Boston Massachusetts on the 19th September 1969 and several souvenir covers were produced to record this event.

The souvenir cover below, cancelled at the Festiniog Railway was to be carried be carried throughout the planned tour and carries the SS Saxonia cachet for the sailing on 19 September and the Houston, tour closing cachet alongside the Festiniog railway cachet and stamp. The cover was to be collected at Minfforfd station at the close of the tour Whether it stayed with the locomotive and went to Canada is unknown.

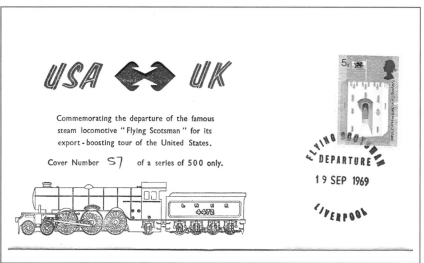

The above two souvenir covers are examples of the different types that can be found, and illustrate the immense interest shown in the locomotive leaving.

A brief overall description of the tour

Following overhaul in the winter of 1968–69 Harold Wilson's government agreed to support Alan

Pegler running the locomotive in the United States and Canada to support British exports. To

comply with local railway regulations it was fitted with: a cowcatcher, bell, buckeye couplings,

American-style whistle, air brakes, and high-intensity headlamp. After a 10 day voyage to Boston,

Massachusetts,the tour started but ran into immediate problems, with some states increasing costs

by requiring diesel-headed-haulage through them, seeing the locomotive as a fire-hazard.

However, the train ran from Boston to New York, Washington and Dallas in 1969; from Texas to

Wisconsin and finishing in Montreal in 1970; and from Toronto to San Francisco in 1971 — a total

of 15,400 miles (24,800 km).

Government financial support for the tour was withdrawn by Prime Minister Edward Heath's

Conservative government in 1970, but Alan Pegler decided to return for the 1970 season. By the

end of that season's tour, the money had run out and Pegler was £132,000 in debt, with the

locomotive in storage at the US Army Sharpe Depot to keep it away from unpaid creditors.Alan

Pegler worked his passage home from San Francisco to England on a P&O cruise ship in 1971,

giving lectures about trains and travel; he was declared bankrupt in the High Court in 1972.

Below is an example of the first souvenir covers carried from Boston to Hartford Connecticut.on the

13th of October 1969, on a trial run, before the official start of the tour.

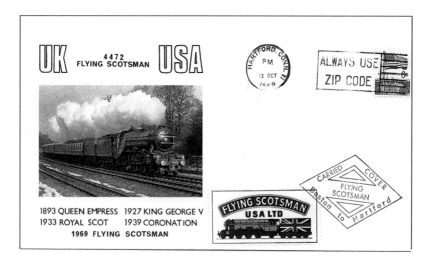

Souvenir Covers were produced for each stage of the tour

of the Eastern States

All the official carried covers were the same design but the post marks and carried cachet were of course different. I will therefore try to follow the route with the covers in my collection, to demonstrate the concept. I will then provide copies of the post marks and journey cachets from the ones that are fairly standard , so here we go with a cover post marked in Boston for the Tour opening and journey to New York, were it was on the 17th of October. The New York covers on the following page are a different type from the main covers used for the tour.

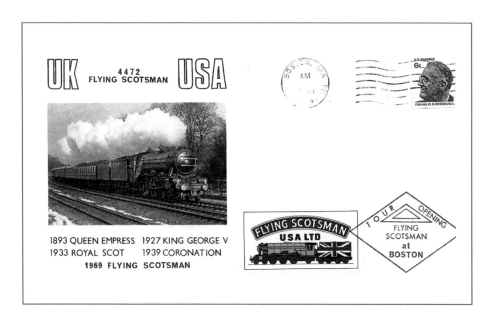

NEW YORK CITY WELCOMES the legendary
Flying Scotsman, the first steam locomotive of
Great Britain to officially break the 100 miles
per hour record 35 years ago. Will tour the
U.S.A. with nine cars filled with a wide range
of products and services from both American
and British firms.

C. SARZIN
PORT WASHINGTON
L. I., NEW YORK

The New York covers are different and again in philatelic terms different printings

NEW YORK CITY WELCOMES the legendary
Flying Scotsman, the first steam locomotive of
Great Britain to officially break the 100 miles
per hour record 35 years ago. Will tour the
U.S.A. with nine cars filled with a wide range
of products and services from both American
and British firms.

C. SARZIN
PORT WASHINGTON
L. I., NEW YORK

Covers for the visits to Philadelphia and Baltimore, on October 21st and 24th 1969.

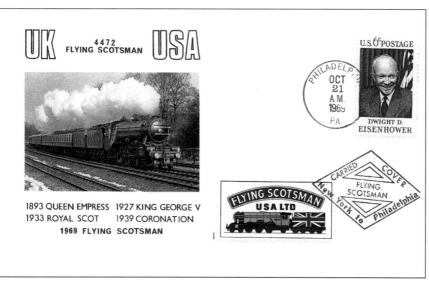

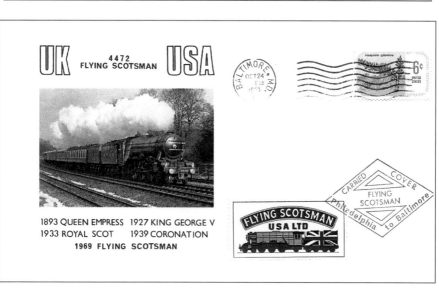

The covers continue to be the same for the rest of the tour except for the post mark and cachet. I will therefore only show this aspect of the covers except for any major differences.

The postmarks above are of destinations between Baltimore and Houston where the original tour was planned to end as can be seen illustrated by the relevant souvenir covers.

The above cover featured at the start of this section and I wondered if, that when the cover was collected at Minfforfd station at the close of the tour,whether it would have stayed with the locomotive and gone to Canada.

I would suggest that as the cover has the Houston tour closing cachet it would have been returned, by post with other covers at the close of the original tour.

The cover below is included only because it is the only one I have seen with the carried from Hartford to New York i.e. Via Boston. The tour to Hartford being the trial run. The cover wasn't posted until October 28th by which time Flying Scotsman was in Washington, a puzzle or just forgetfulness

1970 CANADIAN TOUR.

As has been stated before the Government financial support for the tour was withdrawn by Prime Minister Edward Heath's Conservative government in 1970, but Alan Pegler decided to return for the 1970 season. Flying Scotsman Enterprises was formed with George Hinchcliffe as general manager. Finances were not good but the tour went ahead. Flying Scotsman traveled from Texas to the US National Railroad Museum at Green Bay Wisconsin.

I list again here the tour dates as an aide de memoir of the dates of postal cancellations on the foregoing U.S.A Tour souvenir covers.

Liverpool 19 September 1969

Hartford. 13 October 1969

Boston. 16 October 1969

New York. 17 October 1969

Philadelphia. 21 October 1969

Baltimore. 24. October 1969

Washington 27. October 1969

Atlanta. 31. October 1969

Anniston Atlanta. 2 November 1969

Dallas. 7 November 1969

Fort Worth. 8 November 1969

Houston. 14 November 1969 Original Tour Closing.

I also add the post mark dates of the following Canadian Tour souvenir covers

Canada 1970

Green Bay.

Exhibition Post Office. 13 August 1970. 28. August 1970

Toronto. National Rail Museum 3 September 1970

Ottawa. 18. September 1970

Montreal. 25 September 1970

Kingston Ontario 29 September 1970

Hamilton Ontario. 1 October 1970

Niagara. 3. October 1970

Niagara. 4 October 1970

Covers from Green Bay and the 2nd tour in Canada from August to October in 1970

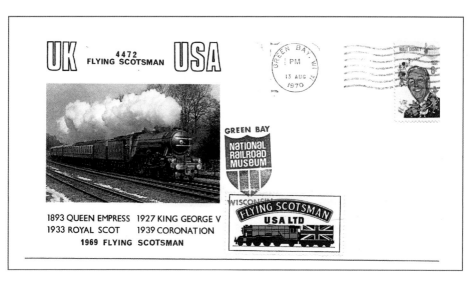

The cover below cancelled on the same day as the cover above celebrates the visit of 4472 to the US National Railway museum in Green Bay but is a very attractive variation and shows ,in addition to illustrations of locomotives in the museum, a picture of 4472 in its American guise with cowcatcher, bell etc as described previously

Flying Scotsman ran from Texas to Wisconsin and finished in Montreal in 1970; and from Toronto to San Francisco in 1971.During the planning of the second tour Alan Pegler received an invitation for Flying Scotsman to take part in the Canadian National Exhibition. The covers below were cancelled at the exhibition post office in Toronto and bear the cachet for the exhibitions post office and for Flying Scotsman's visit

Post card with the Canadian National exhibition cachet.

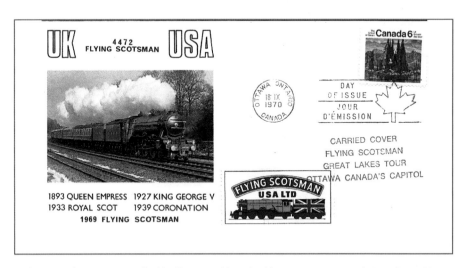

A souvenir cover cancelled in Ottawa with a dual language post mark together with a Great Lakes Tour cachet. This was after Flying Scotsman had spent 10 days at the Toronto exhibition and the Canadian Tour began in earnest.

The next visit was to Montreal. On the 25th of September 1970. The souvenir cover bears a cachet in French.

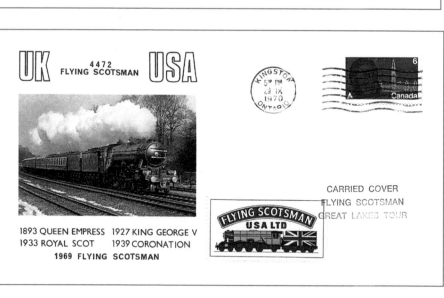

The cover above was cancelled in Kingston on the 29th of October and the following cover 2 days later in Hamilton.

4472
FLYING SCOTSMAN

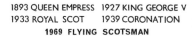

1893 QUEEN EMPRESS   1927 KING GEORGE V
1933 ROYAL SCOT   1939 CORONATION
1969 FLYING SCOTSMAN

CARRIED COVER
FLYING SCOTSMAN
GREAT LAKES TOUR

The following covers are all cancelled at Niagara Falls, but in true philatelic tradition for differences no matter how small, they are all different, the first two both have the same stamps, cancelled at the same time and date, but the carried on board cachets are of different colours.

4472
FLYING SCOTSMAN

BUY
CANADA SAVINGS
BONDS

1893 QUEEN EMPRESS   1927 KING GEORGE V
1933 ROYAL SCOT   1939 CORONATION
1969 FLYING SCOTSMAN

Carried
ON BOARD
Flying Scotsman

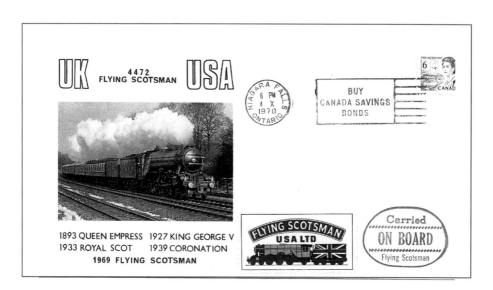

The third cover is completely different both cover and stamp being different, and the Ontario Canadian cancellation a day earlier. The cover also bears a further tour cachet for the visit to Niagara Falls.

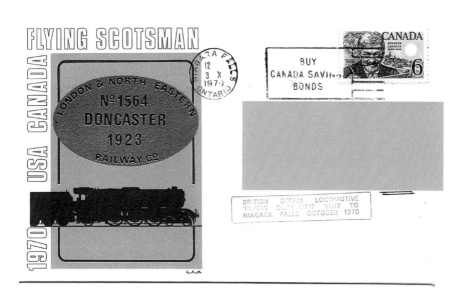

The cover below, denoting the end of the Canadian Tour, is again the same design as the last but has a completely different Niagara Falls, New York U.S.A post mark for the 5th of October 1970.

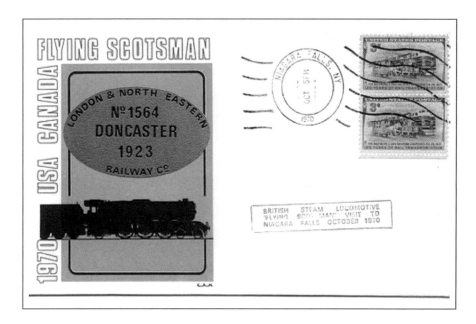

After leaving Niagara Falls it was decided to see if Flying Scotsman's fortunes would improve by spending the following summer in California culminating in British Week in San Francisco. 4472 crossed America via the northern route through the Rocky Mountains then south to San Francisco.

The cover reproduced below is the only cover I have seen dated in 1971 after the Canadian tour. It is also the only one I have seen cancelled in California on the west coast where 4472 ended up in San Francisco. It does not have a journey cachet and was probably not carried. The cover is however another philatelic puzzle.

After a very difficult journey all that happened in San Francisco was a static exhibition at Fishermans Wharf followed by a 2 mile, back and forth journey along the waterfront.

Flying Scotsman was then placed in storage, for safe keeping, until the well recorded rescue by Sir William McAlpine. I have never seen any philatelic material from this period of 4472's preservation.

During the time that Flying Scotsman was in the U.S.A it was not forgotten by the philatelic trade and organisations back home in the UK. As is shown by the following two covers.

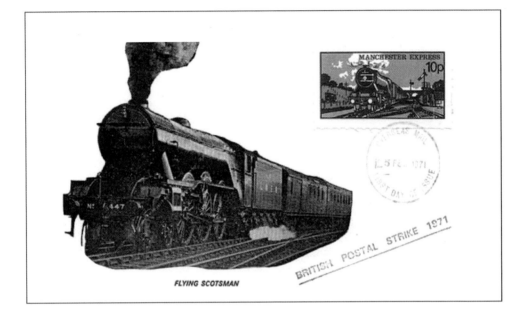

FLYING SCOTSMAN

The cover above was issued during the 1971 postal strike and used images of Flying Scotsman on both the covers and stamps to enhance its Manchester Express private local mail.

The cover below one of a series issue using British National Railway Museums covers, used on the American tour carried on various Traveling Post Offices. This one was carried and cancelled on a Down Special TPO.

BRITISH NATIONAL RAILWAY MUSEUMS
COMMEMORATE THE VISIT OF 4472 TO A.N.R.M

AMERICAN NATIONAL RAILROAD MUSEUM

E.W.Laver
Opposite The Church
Weston Longville
Norwich
NOR 59X

THE McALPINE YEARS

Fears then arose for the engine's future, the speculation being that it might remain in the US or even be broken up. After Alan Bloom made a personal phone call to him in January 1973, William McAlpine stepped in and bought the locomotive for £25,000 direct from the finance company in San Francisco docks.This story has been well documented so I won't retell it.

After its return to the UK via the Panama Canal in February 1973, McAlpine paid for the locomotive's restoration at Derby Works. The cover below was. Issued to welcome Flying Scotsman home to Liverpool.

Trial runs took place on the Paignton and Dartmouth Steam Railway in summer 1973, after which it was transferred to Steamtown (Carnforth), from where it steamed on various tours. In December 1977 'Flying Scotsman' entered the Vickers Engineering Works, Barrow-in-Furness for heavy repairs, including an unused replacement boiler.

I have not seen any covers of the original the 1973 visit to the Paignton and Dartmouth but in 1993 to Flying Scotsman visited again and souvenir covers and certificates were produced and are reproduced above and over the page to celebrate the 20th anniversary.

20th ANNIVERSARY VISIT
of the famous
FLYING SCOTSMAN

THE NATIONS HOLIDAY LINE

JULY and
AUGUST
1993

PAIGNTON and DARTMOUTH STEAM RAILWAY
Certificate number....00003793....
Certified that..travelled behind the
FLYING SCOTSMAN in.................................1993

Chairman
Paignton and Dartmouth Steam Railway

P & D S R   SOUVENIR OF: FLYING SCOTSMAN
             20TH ANNIVERSARY   B.R.
                 1973-1993   60103

Posted on board the first ever post office on a preserved standard
gauge railway hauled by B.R. 60103 FLYING SCOTSMAN.

The above items are out of chronological sequence but are evidence of the fact that the visit was

still remembered 20 years later and beyond. The Postcard above however is a photograph taken in

Kingswear at the time

Other items in my collection from the early McAlpine years are shown now. Firstly souvenir covers celebrating the locomotives 50th anniversary on May 2nd 1973.

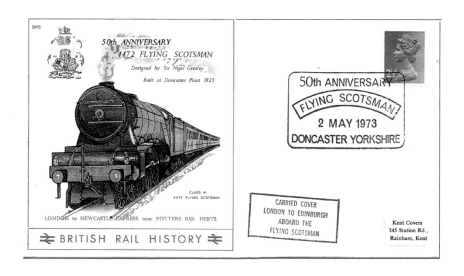

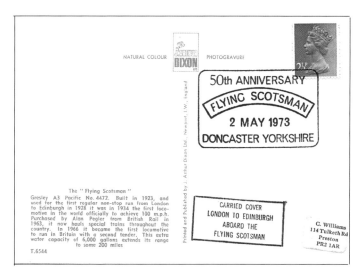

The first cover was issued as part of a series to celebrate British Rail History and bears the cachet that it was carried aboard the Flying Scotsman.The second cancellation and cachet is the same but is on the reverse of a Flying Scotsman postcard.

The following two covers were produced by different companies for the same event , the open day

at the Birmingham Railway Museum at Tyseley In 1973. Flying Scotsman was of course the star attraction. The two covers contain inserts that detail the history and achievements of Flying Scotsman so I reproduce them here.

PRESERVED LOCOMOTIVE SERIES
PLS 18 BIRMINGHAM RAILWAY MUSEUM

The Birmingham Railway Museum is sited in the British Railway Diesel Depot at Tyseley, the buildings incorporate a purpose built maintenance and repair shop together with the old steam depot coaling plant converted into furthe storage space. A very representative range of steam locomotives are housed at Tyseley and work is actively carried out on restoring several steam locos to full working order as well as the maintenance of steam locomotives used to haul special trains on British Railways.

The Open Day this year features 4472 Flying Scotsman the most famous locomotive in the world. Built at the Doncaster Plant of the L.N.E.R. in 1923 as the third of Sir Nigel Gresley's A1 pacific class she was the first loco to officially record a speed of 100 mph verified from dynamometer car readings on the 23rd November 1934 while desending Stoke Bank with a train of 6 coaches weighing 207 tons.

The cover shows 4472 as she ran in her tour of the United States and Canada in 1969 to 1972 when she toured with a train of British coaches. The bell was presented by the Southern Railway of the USA and is the only piece of the equipment still carried,the large whistle,headlamp and ' pilot ' (cowcatcher) are now removed. 4472 travelled over 12,000 miles in the States without any major fault developing - a fine achievement for a locomotive then almost 50 years old.

FLYING SCOTSMAN COMMEMORATIVE COVER

FLYING SCOTSMAN AT TYSELEY, 7th. OCTOBER, 1973

Birmingham Steam Museum, on the site of the Tyseley motive power depot, is a museum-workshop conceived specifically for the maintenance of preserved steam locomotives to main line standards. Its layout is such that the visitor may see not only the locomotives, but the detail of their routine operation. The depot is itself a record of industrial archaeology.

Star attraction at the steam Open Day on 7th. October, 1973, is "Flying Scotsman", best-known and most widely travelled of British locomotives. If locomotives can be said to have personalities, then "F.S." has certainly led an adventurous life:

Feb. 1923	Completed at Doncaster works, 3rd. of the Gresley "Pacifics", and the first completed under the newly-formed LNER. Named after the London-Edinburgh train which had run since 1862.
1924	On show at the British Empire Exhibition, Wembley, alongside GWR "Caerphilly Castle". This resulted in the famous challenge match between the two classes of loco.
1st May, 1928	First non-stop run of "Flying Scotsman" train from London to Edinburgh, 392.7 miles. (The LMS stole the thunder by running the "Royal Scot", specially lightened, non-stop the previous day).
1928	"Flying Scotsman" the star of a feature film: that the plot is puerile is beside the point!
Nov. 30th. 1934	In the course of a high speed test from London to Leeds and return, "Flying Scotsman" was credited with 100 m.p.h., the first time this figure had been "officially confirmed" for a British locomotive. (It had been claimed for GWR "City of Truro" in 1904, and approved and disproved many times since. Even the dynamometer record of "Flying Scotsman's" run has been called into question by at least one eminent observer. But these academic arguments do not detract from the significance of either event.)
Jan. 14th 1964	Last run in British Railways service. Bought directly out of traffic by Mr. Alan Pegler. Restored to LNER livery, with single chimney. First special runs later the same year.
1968	"Flying Scotsman" the only engine to escape B.R. ban on special steam workings: roamed to many parts of the country far from its native east coast main line. Now coupled to two tenders, for independence from external water supplies.
1st May 1968	40th. anniversary of the first non-stop London-Edinburgh service. Film of this dramatic run was made for BBC television.
Sept. 1969	"F.S." shipped to U.S.A. to haul British exhibition train. Those who saw her on her last runs in UK, incongruously carrying a bell and American hooter, and prophesied that she would never return were nearly right. Her U.S. travels were fraught with contention, financial and legal problems, and finally bankrupted her owner.
Dec. 1972	Mr. W. McAlpine bought the locomotive to prevent seizure by three U.S. railroads for non-payment of dues. "Flying Scotsman" shipped (rather surreptitiously) back to Liverpool.
Feb. 18th 1973	Triumphant progress under her own steam to Derby for overhaul by British Rail Engineering, prior to resuming special steam workings on B.R. tracks, the steam ban having been lifted during her exile.

The artist's drawing is his first-hand impression of "Flying Scotsman" during its period of operation on the Torbay Steam Railway in the summer of 1973.

SPECIAL SOUVENIR PLATFORM TICKET

ADMIT ONE

to view the London & North Eastern locomotive No. 4472 "Flying Scotsman" on tour with H. P. Bulmer Ltd.

2 6 SEP 1973

Total weight 161 tons 4 cwt in working order.	Water capacity 5000 gals.
	Coal capacity 9 tons.
Length 70' 2⅜"	Boiler pressure 220 lbs per
Tractive effort 32,910 lbs.	square inch.
Driving wheels 6' 8"	Cylinders (3) 19" x 26"

Price 10p   N⁰ 13611

The above souvenir platform ticket was

from when 4472 was on tour with H.P.

Bulmer the cider makers in September

1973

From August 1st to August 10th Flying Scotsman was on display at Kensington Olympia then transferred to its new base at Steamtown in Carnforth in Lancashire.

The items below, showing both sides of a souvenir platform ticket, are not philatelic but would allowed to be part of a Social philately display and are therefore included in this account.

1899 – 1974

SPECIAL
SOUVENIR
PLATFORM
TICKET

ADMIT ONE

TO VIEW THE L.N.E.R. LOCOMOTIVE No. 4472 "FLYING SCOTSMAN"
on display in conjunction with the
Castrol Great Motoring Extravaganza **1-10 AUGUST 1974**

View also the FREE British Rail "Railways Today – Railways Tomorrow" Exhibtion

Price 10p   № 01236

This ticket does not admit to the exhibition in the National Hall Olympia

---

L.N.E.R. LOCOMOTIVE No. 4472 "FLYING SCOTSMAN" (4 – 6 – 2 Type)

Total weight 161 tons 4 cwt in working order	Water Capacity 5,000 gals
	Coal Capacity 9 tons
Length 70' 2⅜"	Boiler Pressure 220 lbs per square inch.
Tractive Effort 32,910 lbs.	
Driving Wheels 6' 8"	Cylinders (3) 19" x 26"

Designed by Sir Nigel Gresley and built at Doncaster in 1922, Flying Scotsman regularly worked express passenger trains on the East Coast Main Line.

On 1st May, 1928, it became the first locomotive to complete a non stop run between Kings Cross and Edinburgh – the run was repeated on 1st May, 1968! On November 30th, 1934, it became the first locomotive to officially reach 100 mph.

Purchased by W. H. McAlpine in 1973, Flying Scotsman has been restored in Derby Works.

 Issued subject to British Railways Board Bye-Laws and con-
ditions relating to platform tickets. Not valid for travel on trains.

Flying Scotsman was transferred to its new base at Steamtown in Carnforth in

Lancashire after the Olympia display in mid August 1974

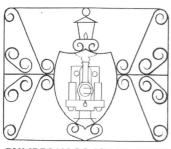

FIRST DAY COVER

CUMBRIAN COAST EXPRESS

Commemorating the second season of
British Rail sponsored Steam-hauled
excursion trains to Ravenglass.
June 26th 1979.

N. G. Withers, Esq.,
Manor House,
Middleton Place,
BOOTLE STATION,
Cumbria

Flying Scotsman ran many tours from Steamtown including regular Cumbrian coast express to

Ravenglass and Selafield as described in my opening comments and illustrated by the cover

above. I include a further personal photograph of 4472 at Ravenglass.

The following images on postcards show various activities undertaken during Flying Scotsman's stay at Carnforth Steamtown, The first showing 4472 being coaled at the coaling tower.

Ex. L.N.E.R. A3 4-6-2 No. 4472 'Flying Scotsman' at Steamtown Railway Museum, Carnforth.   *Photograph by Jeff Colledge*

Alongside is a personal photograph of A4 Sir Nigel Gresley being coaled at the tower taken from the bridge outside Carnforth station, after a long fruitless wait to see 4472 being coaled. It does however link nicely to the next post card.

4472 poses alongside 4498 Sir Nigel Gresley outside the sheds at Steamtown.

Below, Scotsman takes its turn on the internal passenger services to Steamtown.

The following souvenir covers are out of chronological order but as they relate, once again, to the 1985 issue of Great Train commemorative stamps. The covers are produced by various companies but all relate to Flying Scotsman and/or, are cancelled in Carnforth and in one case Doncaster.

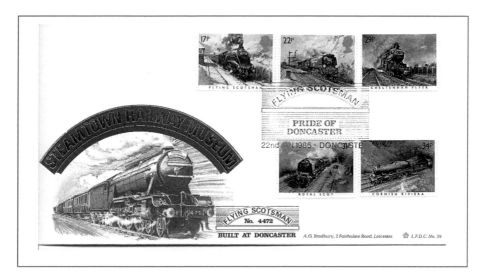

From the 12th of March to June 1980 4472 appeared at the 150th anniversary celebrations of the Liverpool and Manchester Railway. This event was just one of the many that had Flying Scotsman as a celebrity visitor, even when there was no direct connection as in this case.

Between August 1974 and the Exhibition at Olympia ,and the move to Steamtown 4472 had a new smoke box fitted at Carnforth in1975.

In August 1975 the locomotive appeared at the Stockton and Darlington 150th anniversary but to date I have been unable to find any philatelic evidence.

In November 1977 Flying Scotsman appeared with Dustin Hoffman and Vanessa Redgrave in the Warner Brothers Film Agatha as 4474 *Victor Wilde and 4480 Enterprise.*

From December 1977 to June 1978, 4472 was overhauled at Vickers Barrow after running approximately 59,000 miles since July 1973

Below are reproduced both sides of a postcard issued to raise both awareness and funds for the Save the Save the Settle and Carlisle Line. The card depicts 4472 In September 1978 soon after its overhaul.

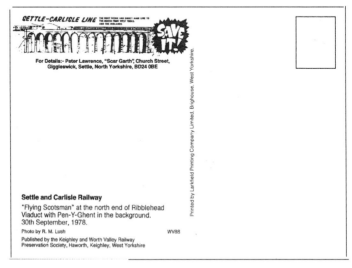

The postcard above, being for the first day of the issue of the Rocket 150 stamps, was carried by Flying Scotsman during the celebrations, as is shown by the cachet. Below is the front of the souvenir postcard.

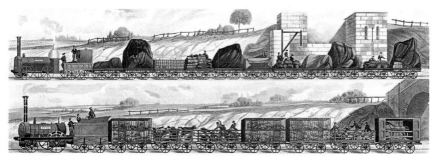

TRAVELLING ON THE LIVERPOOL AND MANCHESTER RAILWAY.

A Train of Waggons, with Goods Ec.Ec.
also
A Train of Carriages, with Cattle.

Nov. 1831.

Throughout the early 1980's Flying Scotsman was gainfully employed hauling tours, and attending as the celebrity locomotive for many celebrations and runs including :-

Between 1982 and 1984 4472 ran with A4 4498's corridor tender in green livery, while a new body was made for it's own tender chassis

February- March 1983 Diamond Jubilee runs including East Coast Main Line from Peterborough to Edinburgh. Electrification of the line from Kings Cross precluding the use of that part of the line.

September 4 1983 unofficially adopted by The Parachute Regiment.

20 November 1984 Hauled the Royal Train for the HM The Queen Mother from Stratford to Woolwich.

Early in 1985 Flying Scotsman attended the Manchester museum of Science and Industry who produced the souvenir postcard below.

March 27 to December 1985, 7 year overhaul at Carnforth including a boiler retube having completed an estimated 135.000 miles since June 1978, then moved to Marylebone. On the 4th April 1987 it was moved to Carnforth. On the 23th August 1987, 4472 ran a charter for Halls Mentholyptus and is depicted below at Hale.

Above is a picture of 4472 assisting class 5 4-6-0 45290 on a Manchester Victoria to Carnforth charter near Entwistle near Bolton in Lancashire. The date is uncertain, but as Carnforth is involved it was probably the mid 1980's.

COALVILLE OPEN DAY
1987

1987 *Bretham* R4

4472 Flying Scotsman

Westcliff House,
Folkestone, Kent

The above cover was possibly one of the last souvenirs before in February 1988 4472 moved to Southall for overhaul in preparation for the Australian tour, The estimated distance run since December 1985 was 13,500 miles. The driving wheels were re-tyred and Air brake and electric lights fitted, and the steam heating and AWS were disconnected.

Flying Scotsman only had one public run in Britain, on the 14th of August, since its overhaul before being shipped from Tilbury to Sydney from 12 September to 16 October 1988 insured for £1,000,000.

A short biography of The Hon. Sir William McAlpine included with the covers signed by him.

The Hon.
Sir William McAlpine

Sir William McAlpine was born in 1936. He started work at 16 ½ and spent all of his life since then in the construction industry. Sir William is the great grandson of Sir Robert McAlpine, 1st Bt. founder of the world famous Sir Robert McAlpine, LTD construction company.

Sir William McAlpine is well known for his love of steam trains and owns a large collection of vintage vehicles and steam engines. In 1973, he purchased The Flying Scotsman (illustrated in the Cuneo Painting on the cover he has signed) and continued to maintain her privately for hauling special trains over BR lines and on private railways. Under his ownership, Flying Scotsman set a new world record for a non-stop run for steam by hauling a train for 422 miles from Parkes to Broken Hill in New South Wales.

In 1996, with great sadness, Sir William sold Flying Scotsman to Dr Tony Marchington who took on the complex and very costly responsibility of restoring the locomotive and train back to the highest standard of operational condition.

Sir William is Chairman of the Railway Heritage Trust, President of the Railway Benefit Fund, Chairman of Paignton and Kingswear Railway and Romney Hythe and Dymchurch Railway, President of Transport Trust and Chairman of the Trustees of the Steamship Sir Walter Scott on Loch Katrine.

He is President, Patron, Trustee, Chairman or Director to countless Heritage sector organisations and will be forever synonymous with rescuing the iconic steam locomotive from the US in 1973.
He commissioned from Terence Cuneo the painting of Flying Scotsman which is the background to the stamp sheets.

Information provided by Sir William McAlpine (July 2009)

Visit www.sir-robert-mcalpine.com to learn more.

THE TOUR OF AUSTRALIA TO CELEBRATE THE BI-CENTENNIAL

It had been decided that a railway demonstration should form part of the celebrations because of the importance of the 'iron road' in the development of Australia as a nation.

Melbourne was 4472's first destination in Australia and has both standard and broad gauge.New South Wales, Brisbane and Perth together with Adelaide all have standard gauge together with other gauges so it was possible to visit all these major cities.

Additionally as Australia's first railway locomotives were British it was felt to be important that a British Locomotive was present.

Bill McAlpine agreed to Flying Scotsman could attend after concrete financial agreements were in place for funding the tour and transportation of 4472 to and from Australia.

A souvenir cover celebrating the departure of Flying Scotsman to Australia. The journey from Tilbury, lasted from the 12th of September to the 16th of October 1988 when the locomotive arrived in Sydney.

The above cover is doubled cover i.e. It was cancelled firstly in Doncaster England, where Flying Scotsman was built, before it embarked for Australia. It cancelled again in Doncaster Australia. The cover contained the insert below.

'FLYING SCOTSMAN' VISITS AUSTRALIA

The Bicentennial event Aus Steam 88, incorporating the visit of Flying Scotsman, is to commemorate the involvement of the railways in assisting the development of Australia.

Flying Scotsman represents the British locomotive builders who over the years supplied locomotives to the Australian railways and the engineers and men who helped to build them.

While in Australia, Flying Scotsman may visit every State, except Tasmania, as the standard gauge now links all capital cities and has overcome the problem of change of gauge at each State border.

In visiting Australia, Flying Scotsman will become the first locomotive to circumnavigate the world, travelling by courtesy of P&O via the Cape of Good Hope and returning to England via Cape Horn: this will add to Flying Scotsman being the most famous steam locomotive and, certainly the most travelled.

Built in 1922, she entered service on 27th February 1923 and was named after the LNERs most prestigious train, ready for the 1925 Wembley Exhibition. In 1928 she hauled the first non-stop train from Kings Cross to Edinburgh and repeated the feat 40 years later. In 1934 she achieved an official world record of 100 mph.

In 1963 Flying Scotsman was purchased by Alan Pegler and after running thousands of miles in the UK was shipped to America visiting all the major East Coast cities and crossing the continent to San Francisco. In 1973 she was bought by The Hon. WH McAlpine and shipped back to the UK from Oakland resuming her role as the premier steam locomotive running on British railways.

Commemorative Cover designed and published by CoverCraft, PO Box 713, London, SE19 2HH.

Special handstamps applied by The British Post Office and Australia Post.

Insert card text, courtesy of Mr George Hinchcliffe.

The first revenue earning run in Australia on the 25th of October 1988 is illustrated by the souvenir cover below.

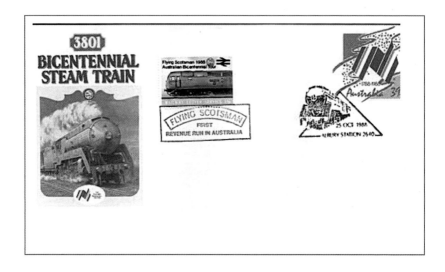

Soon after its arrival in Ausralia, Flying Scotsman was transferred south to Melbourne, Victoria to take part in the Aus' Steam '88 celebrations. It hauled many excursions to Seymour, and return and was also put on display at Spencer Street Station when not on duty. The above cover contained the insert below describing the whole planned Aus' Steam '88 tour.

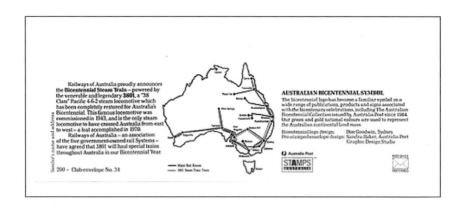

The next souvenir cover welcomed 4472 to Melbourne, Victoria and displays several self explanatory, additional cachets and stamps on the cover bearing a picture of restored 3801

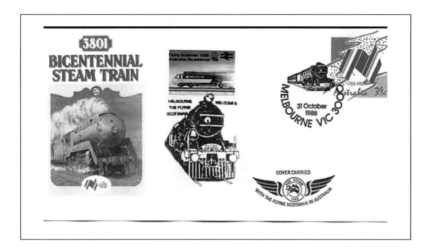

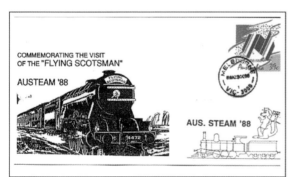

The two covers alongside, and below, are both alternative souvenirs of the Melbourne visit

After a very successful tour of Victoria and Flying Scotsman was then moved north to New South

Wales, from Dec 1988 to March 1989, were the standard gauge system offered a great deal more

variety for tours and the opportunity was taken to visit many destinations also it should be noted

here that it toured with preserved class 38 Pacific No 3801. The A3 was mainly based in Sydney.

Brisbane in March 1989, Thirlmere Railway, and Coulbourn were also on the agenda, some of

which are illustrated by the souvenir covers below. Over a long weekend from 9-12 June 1989 the

two locomotives visited Dubbo and then did a return trip to Orange, before returning to Sydney,

illustrated on the following pages showing both sides of the souvenir cover from the Dubbo

weekend.

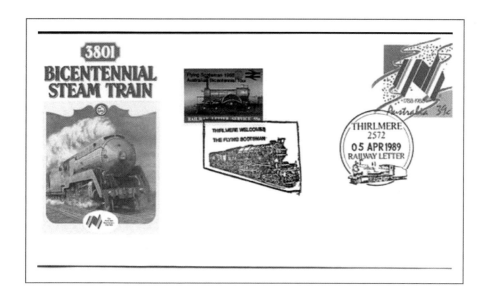

The above cover celebrates a visit to the Thirlmere Railway museum, a visit unusual in that the railway also issued a miniature sheet of Flying Scotsman souvenir railway stamps.

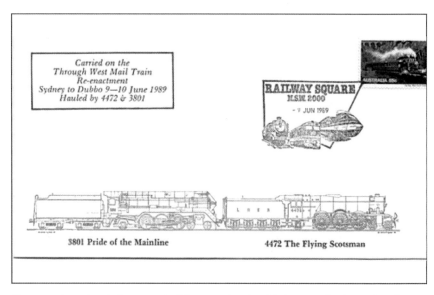

3801 Pride of the Mainline   4472 The Flying Scotsman

The cover shown here is the souvenir of the reenactment mail train as previously mentioned.

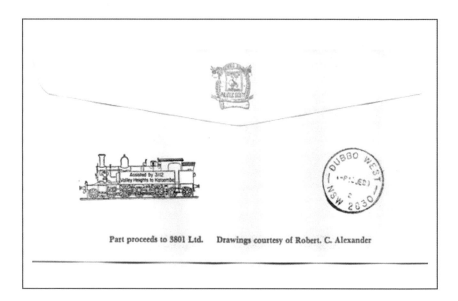

Part proceeds to 3801 Ltd.   Drawings courtesy of Robert. C. Alexander

The 6th of August 1989 saw the start of the legendary tour to Alice Springs the tour was itemised on the insert to the souvenir covers that now had a different design. The insert is shown below.

```
                            FLYING SCOTSMAN
-----------------------------------------------------------------------
Sun   Aug.6        dep Melbourne            Sun   Aug.20 dept Alice Springs
          overnight Cootamundra             Mon   Aug.21 In Transit - Pt.August
Mon   Aug.7   Cootamundra - Parkes          Tue   Aug.22 Port Augusta
Tue   Aug.8   Parkes - Broken Hill          Wed   Aug.23 Adelaide
Wed   Aug.9   Broken Hill - P'boro          Thu   Aug.24 Adelaide
Thur  Aug.10  P'boro - Pt.Augusta           Fri   Aug.25 Adelaide
Fri   Aug.11  Port Augusta                  Sat   Aug.26 Adelaide
Sat   Aug.12  Port Augusta                  Sun   Aug.27 Adelaide
Sun   Aug.13  dep Pt.Augusta                Mon   Aug.28 dept Adelaide - P'boro
Mon   Aug.14  In Transit - Alice Springs    Tue   Aug.29 P'boro - Broken Hill
Tue   Aug.15  Alice Springs                 Wed   Aug.30 Broken Hill - Parkes
Wed   Aug.16  Alice Springs                 Thu   Aug.31 Parkes - Bathurst
Thu   Aug.17  Alice Springs                 Fri   Sep.1  Bathurst - Sydney
Fri   Aug.18  Alice Springs                 Sat   Sep.2  Sydney - Melbourne
Sat   Aug.19  Alice Springs
          Run with restored GHAN
```

There now follows examples of the covers from this part of the tour, the first being cancelled at Port Augusta Philatelic Centre on the 10th of August when 4472 had arrived from Peterborough. On the 8th of August the journey from Parkes to Broken Hill a distance of 422 miles 7.59 chains was covered in 9 hours 25m minutes 4.46 seconds, hauling 535 tons gross. A new world record for steam traction. Unfortunately I have never seen a cover for sale covering this event.

At Port Augusta 4472 was prepared for it's journey across the dessert to Alice Springs and so became the first standard gauge steam locomotive to do so. Flying Scotsman arrived in Alice Springs on August 14th, and stayed until the 19th when it ran with the restored Ghan.

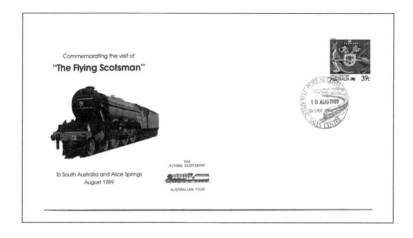

A souvenir cover for the visit to Peterborough. South Australia.

And now a cover for the visit to Alice Springs, the post mark depicting The Ghan and 4472. The Flying Scotsman tour stamp appears in red, previous covers have it in blue and green.

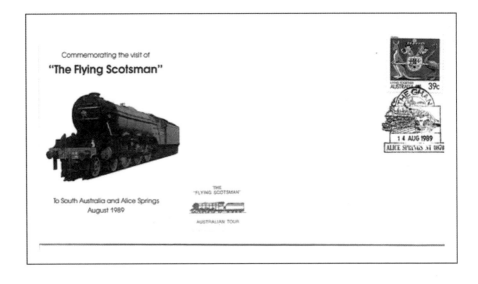

A postcard issued for the Australian tour, cancelled in Alice Springs and showing reverse below.

POST CARD

VISIT OF "THE FLYING SCOTSMAN" TO AUSTRALIA

After its mammoth journey to Alice Springs, 4472 then returned south to Adelaide and was used for several excursions as well as parallel running with two former South Australian Railway broad gauge locomotives before returning once more to Sydney on August 28th.

The very last stage of the Australian adventure ' The West Australian ' where 4472 was to cross the entire Australian continent from Sydney to Perth a distance of 2461 miles and made its destination just 9 minutes late. The highlight of its visit to Perth was a reunion with GWR No 4079 Pendennis Castle that had arrived in Perth on September 4th. The reunion taking place on September 17th.

Commemorating the visit of
"The Flying Scotsman"

To South Australia and Alice Springs
August 1989
Western Australia
September - October
1989

The above cover cancelled in Perth signalled the end of the tour and Flying Scotsman steamed back to Sydney to be loaded aboard the French vessel *La Perouse,* the ship leaving for Tilbury via New Zealand and Cape Horn on November 12th, arriving Thursday December 14th.

Flying Scotsman was moved to Southall where Roland Kennington the CME inspected and overhauled 4472 over a period of 3 months?

During 1990 the locomotive was temporarily based at Crewe and ran a several trips to Holyhead. Later in the year Flying Scotsman took part, with other preserved locomotives, in running trains on the Severn Valley Railway to celebrate it's 25 year of running since restoration.

A major problem would have to be overcome by the end of October 1992 when 4472's main line safety certificate would expire. This however did not apply to running on privately owned heritage and preserved lines.

The decision to make the loco available for hire involved moving from it from one location to another by road low-loader.

From October 26th to the 1st of December 1992 Flying Scotsman was at the Tyseley shed of the Birmingham Railway Museum when it was decided to offer the opportunity of driving the engine to the public.

Later visits were made to the Great Central Railway in Loughborough from December 3rd 1992 to the 29th of January 1993 and from 31st of January to March 2nd at the East Lancashire Railway in Bury, where I had personal experience of the visit. I will describe in the next section.

I have unfortunately, not found any philatelic evidence of the period from 1990 to the end of 1992, but as I have mentioned before , ephemera related to a subject in a philatelic exhibit would be allowed.

1993 VISITS TO PRIVATE RAILWAYS INCLUDING THE VISIT TO THE EAST LANCASHIRE RAILWAY

The following is an account of 4472's visit to the East Lancashire Railway. Please excuse this very personal account of very memorable experiences that describe my view of the visit. The first of which was seeing it arrive on a low lower and being unloaded in Castlecroft yard in Bury.

31st Jan.

Your chance to drive Flying Scotsman!

● Steaming in, the famous Flying Scotsman

By GAYLE McBAIN

TRAIN buffs will get the chance to fulfil the dream of a lifetime with a visit by the world-famous Flying Scotsman.

And for the real enthusiasts there will be the chance to take a two hour driving course — at a cost of £130.-

The lessons are to be run in February at the East Lancashire Railway.

And organisers, "Adventures in Steam", believe interest will be high.

During the whole of February the engine will be at the railway taking part in the normal weekend scheduled passenger train services.

Trains pulled by the Scotsman will also be available for charter hire during the week, Monday, February 15 to Friday, February 19.

And regular weekday passenger services, with the Scotsman leading the way up the track, will be held throughout the week of Monday, February 22.

Anyone interested in booking should contact Adventures in Steam, on 021-705 8105.

The above newspaper cutting was the first local announcement of Flying Scotsman's visit to the ELR and was seen by my wife who kept it away from me and arranged, what was to be a birthday surprise. It was an amazing surprise however when she had to tell me I was going to drive 4472 and had to sign a disclaimer before the event. Below is a postcard issued after the visit to the East Lancashire Railway.

4472 arrives at Castlecroft yard on the East Lancashire Railway, after being unloaded from the low loader it is moved towards its tender by the diesel shunter.

And below is coupled to it's tender already filled with coal.

Once the locomotive is connected to it's tender it sits ready for duty outside Castlecroft shed

And, below, is welcomed, by GWR "Castle" Nunney Castle passing with an ELR service train to Rawtenstall via Ramsbottom

Tues the 11th of February arrived and clad in boots, boiler suit, and industrial gloves I arrived at Bury Bolton Street station with the voucher below to experience a steam enthusiasts dream of, not only driving a a steam locomotive but driving the worlds favourite locomotive 4472.

FLYING SCOTSMAN DRIVING COURSE

This voucher entitles...ALAN RIGBY............ to attend a two hour Driver Participation Course on board THE FLYING SCOTSMAN

Adventures in Steam

AT

East Lancashire Railway
Bolton Street Station
Bury, Lancashire

ON

Thursday...11th February, 1993

BETWEEN

1.30 PM. and 3.30 PM

Below I receive my instructions from the driver/ instructor before being allowed on the regulator.

At last the magic moment, hand on the regulator, to begin my driving experience.

As is well known after its stay on the ELR , 4472 was to operate at the Llangollen Railway but was failed, having leaking tubes, and I was therefore one of the last members of the public to ever have this experience, and receive the certificate below

A flyer available at all the ELR stations advertising the visit to Bury.

East Lancashire Railway

Bolton Street Station, Bury, Lancs. BL9 0EY. Telephone: 061-764 7790

Tel: 061-705 5111 weekdays
061-764 7790 weekends

MID WEEK
RUNNING FOR
SCOTSMAN
FEBRUARY
22ND TO 26TH

The Flying Scotsman
will be here!
February 1993

BURY—RAMSBOTTOM—RAWTENSTALL
Operates every weekend in February

The visit was not of course, just about the driving experience but also a full timetable of working ELR service trains that I reproduce below. Flying Scotsman was definitely expected to earn her keep. Below is a photograph of it doing just that at Irwell Vale halt with a Rawtenstall service.

East Lancashire Railway
Bolton Street Station, Bury, Lancs. BL8 0EY. Telephone: 061-764 7790

Flying Scotsman Timetable

ALL TRAINS SHOWN BELOW ARE HAULED BY 'FLYING SCOTSMAN'

SATURDAYS and SUNDAYS in FEBRUARY

BURY	depart	10.00	12.00	2.00	4.00
SUMMERSEAT	depart	10.12	12.12	2.12	4.12
RAMSBOTTOM	arrive	10.18	12.18	2.18	4.18
RAMSBOTTOM	depart	10.25	12.25	2.25	4.25
IRWELL VALE	depart	10.33	12.33	2.33	4.33
RAWTENSTALL	arrive	10.45	12.45	2.45	4.45

RAWTENSTALL	depart	11.00	1.00	3.00	5.00
IRWELL VALE	depart	11.10	1.10	3.10	5.10
RAMSBOTTOM	arrive	11.19	1.19	3.19	5.19
RAMSBOTTOM	depart	11.30	1.30	3.30	5.30
SUMMERSEAT	depart	11.36	1.36	3.36	5.36
BURY	arrive	11.47	1.47	3.47	5.47

and daily from
MONDAY 22nd to FRIDAY 26th FEBRUARY

BURY	depart	10.30	12.30	2.30
SUMMERSEAT	depart	10.42	12.42	2.42
RAMSBOTTOM	arrive	10.48	12.48	2.48
RAMSBOTTOM	depart	10.55	12.55	2.55
IRWELL VALE	depart	11.03	1.03	2.03
RAWTENSTALL	arrive	11.15	1.15	2.15

RAWTENSTALL	depart	11.30	1.30	3.30
IRWELL VALE	depart	11.40	1.40	3.40
RAMSBOTTOM	arrive	11.49	1.49	3.49
RAMSBOTTOM	depart	12.00	2.00	4.00
SUMMERSEAT	depart	12.06	2.06	4.06
BURY	arrive	12.17	2.17	4.17

PLEASE NOTE THAT WHILST EVERY EFFORT IS MADE TO ADHERE TO THE PUBLISHED TIMETABLE THE COMPANY RESERVES THE RIGHT TO MAKE CHANGES WITHOUT NOTICE

Below is how the failure of 4472 was announced by the Times of March 6th 1993.

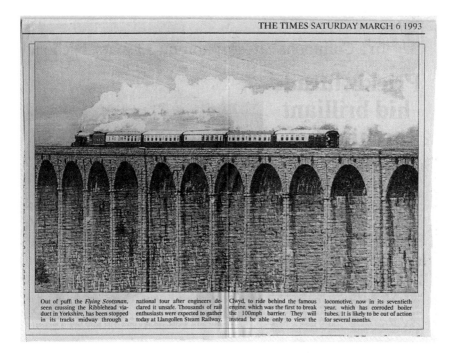

THE TIMES SATURDAY MARCH 6 1993

Out of puff: the *Flying Scotsman*, seen crossing the Ribblehead viaduct in Yorkshire, has been stopped in its tracks midway through a national tour after engineers declared it unsafe. Thousands of rail enthusiasts were expected to gather today at Llangollen Steam Railway, Clwyd, to ride behind the famous engine, which was the first to break the 100mph barrier. They will instead be able only to view the locomotive, now in its seventieth year, which has corroded boiler tubes. It is likely to be out of action for several months.

From April to July 1993 4472 was overhauled by Babcock Robey Ltd. A new exhaust system was fitted along with a new chimney, A boiler retube and a new smoke box was fitted together with German style smoke deflectors. Flying Scotsman was outshopped in BR Brunswick Green and the running number was changed to 60103, the livery and number it had during its final days with BR.

From the 25th July to the 14th September 1993. 60103 recommenced it's tour of private railways at the Paignton and Dartmouth Railway after being transported by road. (See over the page)

The Souvenir cover for this visit was written about earlier in this philatelic account of the locomotive in preservation.

A newspaper cutting shows Flying Scotsman being transported by road to Paignton.

NEWS

RAIL THING: The Flying Scotsman getting a lift on the M5 yesterday

The Flying Scot's on road back

THE Flying Scotsman made a comeback yesterday ... but not under its own steam. The 70-year-old legend — the first British locomotive to be clocked at 100mph — had a police escort as it crawled down the M5 at 20mph on the back of a lorry after having a refit at Oldbury in the West Midlands. The train, withdrawn by British Rail 30 years ago, is expected to be thrilling tourists again on the private Torbay and Dartmouth railway, in Devon, later this week.

Below are personal photographs from my personal collection of 60103 being unloaded at the Paignton and Dartmouth Railway.

21st September 1993 Flying Scotsman Enterprises and Waterman Railways merged to form Flying Scotsman Railways. Pete Waterman becomes joint owner of the locomotive with Sir William McAlpine

From September 1993 to June 1995 The locomotive continued its programs of visits to preserved railways, visiting The Gloucester and Warwickshire Railway, The Birmingham Railway Museum, twice, Llangollen Railway twice, and the Nene Valley Railway, Swanage Railway, and Severn Valley Railway. Before being withdrawn due cracked firebox,moved eventually to Southall Depot. June 1995 locomotive dismantling authorised, ready for major overhaul,

Even though Flying Scotsman visited six preserved railways over the two years, to date I have not found any philatelic material related to the visits.

However I do have a postcard of 4472 on the Settle to Carlisle line at Garsdale with a 1992 charter celebrating Preston Guild 1992,(below) one of the last main charters before the locomotive was restricted to preserved lines.

From October 1993 to June 1995 Flying Scotsman visited Birmingham Railway Museum, Llangollen Railway, Swanage Railway, Severn Valley, and the Nene Valley Railway a souvenir cover from its visit here.. The cover celebrates several things Including the fact that the cover was carried on a train hauled by Flying Scotsman, and is signed by Alan Pegler who continued to follow and support 4472 and affectionately called the locomotive "the old girl "

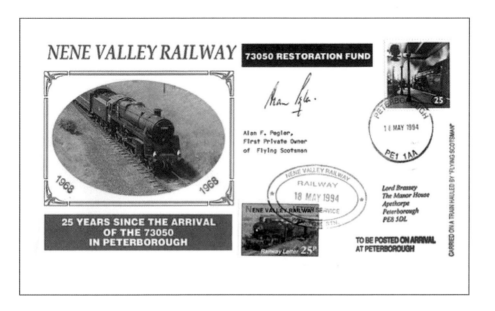

In April 1995 Flying Scotsman was withdrawn due to a cracked firebox and eventually moved to Southall Depot.for major overhaul.

Following are postcards featuring or mentioning Flying Scotsman from my collection that are of LNER interest and are included here from that point of view.

84

THE MARCHINGTON YEARS.

The partnership with Pete Waterman lasted for under two years. When the partnership was over Sir William McAlpine let it be known that after over 20 years of ownership he was willing to sell 4472. This cover signed by Sir William features the Terence Cuneo painting of 4472 and the postmark recognises that it was an official Railway Magazine cover.

Below is a cover signed by Pete Waterman that I include in recognition of his part ownership even though it only reflects his interest in railways but not specifically Flying Scotsman

Dr. Tony Marchington having given Sir William the assurances regarding Flying Scotsman's future, was able to conclude the purchase in March 1996.

Before Flying Scotsman could be used for operational duties the proposed and necessary overhaul had to be completed. Roland Kennington the CME for Sir William for many years and throughout the Australian adventure, was available and willing to take charge of her future. He was reappointed Chief Engineer and with a team of volunteers set about the task of restoration. The covers below (1) signed by Roland Kennington and (2) depicts him firing 4472.

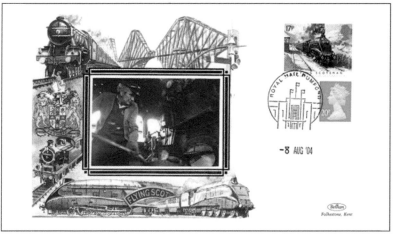

The work of overhaul took Roland Kennington and his team 4 years to complete but at last it was ready to take to the road.

During the time that it took for the major overhaul to be completed Flying Scotsman Railways, as the company, under Tony Marchington, was now named formed the Flying Scotsman Association

to help raise funds for future needs and also keep members informed as to the progress of the overhaul. This was done by the issue of a regular magazine, of which there were eleven over the period of the restoration. Below and alongside, I illustrate, a membership card and the first issue of the magazine. I still have all eleven.

THE OFFICIAL JOURNAL OF THE FLYING SCOTSMAN ASSOCIATION

THE WORLD'S MOST FAMOUS STEAM LOCOMOTIVE

The Flying Scotsman Association Web site home page from 4th May 1999.

The Flying Scotsman Association

This is the official web homepage of the Flying Scotsman Association.

Original artwork by Stuart Black © 1998

Feature	1st May 1928 - 70th Anniversary of the First Non Stop run from London to Edinburgh
News and Noticeboard	Last update April 1999. Flying Scotsman will pull a full public train on 4th July 1999 from Kings Cross to York. See Running Programme for full details of all 15 Flying Scotsman Tours.
Running Programme	Details of the 1999 Public Running Programme for Flying Scotsman
International Gallery	Flying Scotsman in action around the world.
History	A short history of the Flying Scotsman.
Shop	Exclusive memorabilia from the Association.
Membership	Details on how to join the Association.
Overhaul Reports	Jun 96, Nov 96, March 97, Aug 97, Jan 98, Aug 98
Archive	Archive material of old features.
Contacts	Officers of the Association
Links	Other railway sites.

http://www.flyingscotsman.com/fsa.html   04/05/99

The first run albeit in undercoat had been promised to members but in the event had to be cancelled as it was to be a mainline trial instead .Members received an apology from Tony in a letter personally signed by him.

In true philatelic collecting manner the envelope or cover in which a later letter arrived, has been kept and is illustrated below. The cover is Flying Scotsman Railways stationery, as was the letter head. The cancellation is a meter mark.

10th June 1999

Dear Member

Special Train – Saturday 26th June 1999

I am sorry to have to write and tell you that due to final adjustments to Flying Scotsman taking longer than anticipated it will not be possible to run the above train.

I recognise this will be a great disappointment to you but we have made every effort to try and have Flying Scotsman ready for the 26th June. It is most frustrating to miss this date by just one week.

If you wish to have a full refund of the fares you have paid, please let us know and a cheque will be sent to you immediately.

Alternatively we will be prepared to honour your booking on any advertised train in the Flying Scotsman 1999 brochure (except the Millennium Special) for no additional charge providing space is available when you advise us of the train of your choice. As a further option we will allow transfer of the tickets to other persons of your choice.

The first public train hauled by Flying Scotsman will be the Inaugural Scotsman on Sunday 4th July from King's Cross to York.

I am sorry this change of plan has been necessary but I hope you will find the alternatives offered acceptable.

Please telephone Flying Scotsman Railways on 01543-250865 between the hours of 0900 to 1700 Monday to Friday. We look forward to hearing from you.

Yours sincerely

Dr Tony Marchington
Chairman

Soon after however 4472 was to make its first revenue earning run from King's Cross to York on the 4th of July 1999. As I was unable to travel on that train ,but was at York station when she arrived, I made a souvenir cover of my own to record the fact and posted it on York Station.

FLYING SCOTSMAN ASSOCIATION
4472 RETURN TO STEAM

YORK
is a mechanised
Letter Office
PLEASE
USE POSTCODES

THE INAUGURAL SCOTSMAN KINGS CROSS TO
YORK SUNDAY JULY 4TH 1999

POSTED ON YORK
STATION

MR A RIGBY
167 RED LANE
BOLTON
LANCS
BL2 5HP

Souvenir Covers produced for the collector market to mark the event are reproduced here together with a press cutting recording the event.

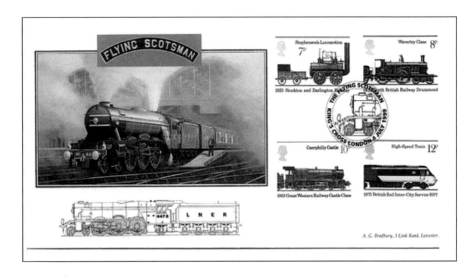

Full steam ahead again for Flying Scotsman

THE Flying Scotsman, the world's most famous steam locomotive, was back on the rails yesterday — and arrived at its destination only 15 minutes late.

The express train made its name with record-breaking runs on the east coast main line in the years before the Second World War and was credited with being the first to break the 100 mph barrier.

Its return follows £1 million of repairs carried out by its owner, Dr Tony Marchington, over three years.

The 76-year-old locomotive steamed out of London's King's Cross station carrying 250 enthusiasts who each paid £350 for a trip to York.

It was ahead of schedule as it approached Doncaster but a broken water pump caused a slight delay.

The train will be on show at the National Railway Museum in York until Sunday.

Back on track: the Flying Scotsman leaves King's Cross station in London yesterday on its journey to York after three years of repairs

Following the inaugural run 4472 ran all over the country heading Pullman Car Trains with titles such as The Eboracun Scotsman or The Shakespeare Scotsman all advertised in a brochure as below. As far as I am aware, that is, I have never seen, any covers that were produced for these trains.

The latter years of Dr Marchington ownership and problems are well documented and beyond the objective of this book.

This personal photograph taken at York after the inaugural run reminds me of the monumental efforts he put in to keep 4472 on the rails.

The next major chapter in the preservation of Flying Scotsman was about to begin.

With the locomotive effectively placed up for sale,by Flying Scotsman Railways and after a national campaign it was bought in April 2004 by the National Railway Museum in York,and it is now part of the museum's National Collection. 4472 was introduced to the public at a ceremonial arrival into the museum during Railfest 200.

Richard Branson was on the footplate in recognition of his generous donation that matched the publics total donations thereby doubling the total.

Unfortunately 4472 broke down on the way to the museum and had to be ignominiously towed into the ceremony by the diesel locomotive Prince William that was also entering the museum's collection on the 29th of May 2004 the above cover was carried on board and also records the fact that it broke down with the addition of a cachet in purple.

After 12 months of interim running repairs, it ran for a while to raise funds for its 10-year restoration. The campaign was " Countdown to back in steam " and then " Ride the Legend " excursions from York to Scarborough. The first of these on was for people who had donated to the purchase fund and my wife and me were fortunate to be on that excursion. As members of the 4472 Association formed by the NRM to keep donators informed of events organised to raise funds for the the major overhaul.

The theme Countdown to back in steam was reflected by the presence of Richard Whitely from TV's Countdown as the honorary guard and gave signal by whistle and green flag to start the train There were no souvenir covers produced, that I am aware of, but I prepared for this eventuality by making some of my own and the cover below was signed by Richard Whitely on arrival in Scarborough.

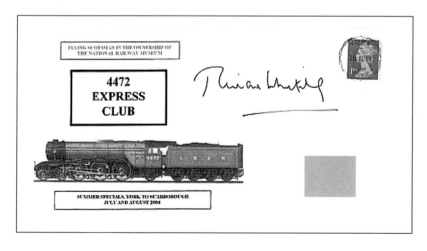

The cover below is one of my treasures because before we left Scarborough I had the privilege to be able to sit and chat with Alan Pegler, on the station in sight of 4472. Before I left him he signed my cover and provided me with a souvenir of a very memorable special day.

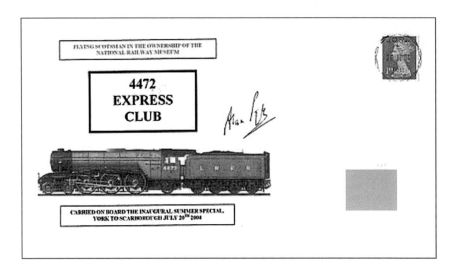

In addition the above signed covers that were cancelled at the main Post office in York I posted the cover below in Scarborough and it was cancelled at York mechanised letter office.

Two souvenirs of my most memorable day our, the ticket and the packed lunch menu.

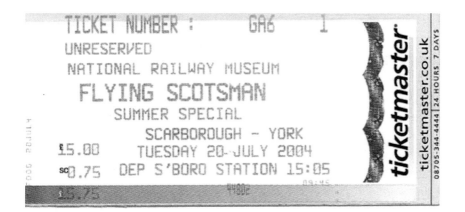

TICKET NUMBER :   GA6   1
UNRESERVED
NATIONAL RAILWAY MUSEUM
FLYING SCOTSMAN
SUMMER SPECIAL
SCARBOROUGH - YORK
£5.00   TUESDAY 20-JULY 2004
sc0.75   DEP S'BORO STATION 15:05
£5.75

milburns

The Flying Scotsman

York to Scarborough 2004

Lunch Menu

Crab, ginger and spring onion mayonnaise with chorizo sausage and rocket in an Alturma bap.

Peppered rare roast beef with fennel coleslaw and horseradish butter in granary bread

Smoked chicken and crispy streaky bacon, black grape and red onion chutney in white bloomer bread

Creamed goats cheese, char-grilled aubergine, sweet peppers, iceberg lettuce and pesto in ciabatta

~~~
Smoked salmon, sour cream and dill frittata

~~~
Mango, pineapple, paw paw and black grape salad with passion fruit and lemongrass syrup

This newspaper cutting shows 4472 on its way to Scarborough with the inaugural Summer Special.

In January 2006, Flying Scotsman entered the National Railway Museum's workshops for a major overhaul to return it to Gresley's original specification and to renew its boiler certificate; originally planned to be completed by mid-2010 if sufficient funds were raised,
In 2011 Donators were invited to the unveiling of the return of Flying Scotsman at the National Railway Museum. Flying Scotsman was presented to invited guests in Wartime black.
After the event there was discovery of additional problems and meant it would not be completed on time.In October 2012, the museum published a report examining the reasons for the delay and additional cost.The locomotive was moved in October 2013 to Bury for work to return it to running condition no earlier than summer 2015. On 29 April 2015, Flying Scotsman's boiler left the National Railway Museum to be reunited with the rest of the locomotive at Riley & Sons in Bury.

The overhaul was completed in January 2016 and testing began on the East Lancashire Railway on 8 January 2016. Flying Scotsman was originally going to haul its inaugural mainline train called the Winter Cumbrian Mountain Express from Manchester Victoria to Carlisle on 23 January, but it was not ready due to faulty brakes.The first mainline run, pulling the Winter Cumbrian Mountain Express from Carnforth to Carlisle, took place on 6 February. An inaugural journey from London King's Cross to York in traditional green livery ran on 25 February. Flying Scotsman will be making special tours throughout the UK in 2016

Below is a reproduction of the National Railway Museum newsletter announcing the Flying Scotsman season programme from February to July 2016

• February – July 2016 •

FLYING SCOTSMAN RETURNS!

A season of events, exhibitions and activities
celebrating the world's most famous locomotive.

For more information:
nrm.org.uk/flyingscotsman

ANNIVERSARIES AND OTHER CELEBRATORY COVERS

Images of Flying Scotsman have been used to celebrate most of its anniversaries and accomplishments and I now include images of some of them that have not been included previously

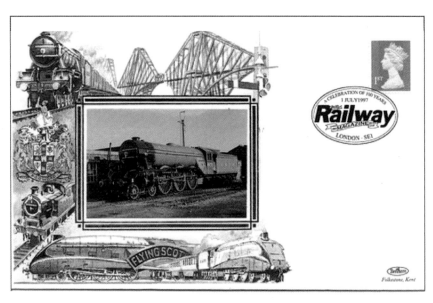

4472 on a cover celebrating one hundred years of the Railway Magazine on 1st July 1997 above and below a similar cover celebrates the 75th anniversary of the first passenger hauling in 1998.

Two similar covers cancelled on the first day of issue in 1999, of the Travellers Tale stamps from the Millennium series of GB commemorative stamps one with the full set and one with a single stamp and signed by Tony Marchington both covers using an image of 4472

A cover to celebrate the 85th Anniversary of Flying Scotsman.

A cover cancelled 1st May 2004 in Edinburgh to celebrate the Anniversary of the first non stop London to Edinburgh on the 1st May 1928

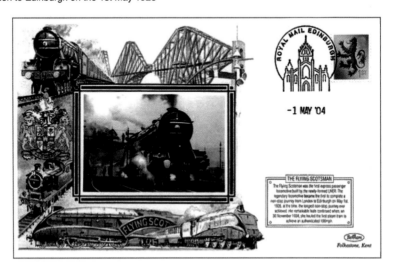

A souvenir cover for the Forth Rail Bridge together with the rear of the cover that explains how, in his own words, Terence Cuneo painted the picture that decorates the cover.

THE FORTH RAIL BRIDGE

Another great bridge recalls somewhat different emotions. In all, I have painted three different scenes of the Forth Bridge, the last, depicting the Flying Scotsman steaming beneath the girders from the north. This was back in the days of Alan Pegler who once owned the engine and was, in fact, the first time the locomotive had ever crossed the Firth. The commission was both amusing and exhilarating. I boarded the engine (which I have been allowed to drive on occasions) at Edinburgh and the four of us, Alan, the driver, the fireman and myself rode her down to the bridge, pulling behind us a single coach containing a number of Alan's friends and assorted goodies of a nutritious and thirst quenching nature.

The form was to drive along the bridge until I felt that we had reached a possible view point. Then, the train would be stopped. I would leap out, run forward and assess the resulting composition. This was the pattern and it went on for quite some time, with me hanging from the cab steps, leaping along the track, shouting to the driver and generally working myself into a state of breathless dedication. Frequently things were rudely interrupted, through the event of another train being signalled, whereupon we would have to reverse briskly back into a siding to allow the wretched thing to pass; then back on to the bridge once more. When, at last, I found the spot I wanted and sat by the trackside sketching away, it became increasingly exasperating to see the Scotsman' suddenly set off backwards, time after time and disappear from sight. However, this is one of the accepted joys of open air work! Eventually the sketch was finished and I was able to retire gratefully to the warmth of the footplate, and on through the corridor in the tender to the coach, where a well earned drink awaited me.

Great Footbridge. Scotsman on the Forth by Terence Cuneo
Copyright The Cuneo Estate

Cover No. 88 of 150

There were many covers produced for the 70th anniversary of the World Steam Record i.e. The fist recorded 100 mph, and I reproduce them here to emphasise the variety available as Flying Scotsman once again became a focus of the publics attention. The first of the following covers was a cover carried on 4472 on its journey to York in May and doubled for the 70th Anniversary in November. The second carried a George V stamp and cachet to record the anniversary.

The following two covers again celebrate the 70th anniversary of the first steam 100mph,the top one also includes two cachets as well as the postmark to mark the anniversary.

The lower cover was a very limited privately produced cover of only I believe 25 Covers.

2004 was quite a year for the issue of covers related to Flying Scotsman, including a First day cover for the new Scottish regional stamps that also was cancelled for the arrival of 4472 at the National Railway Museum

A Railway Magazine cover for the Classic Locomotives miniature sheet also includes a picture of Flying Scotsman by the late Terence Cuneo and is signed by his daughter Carole.

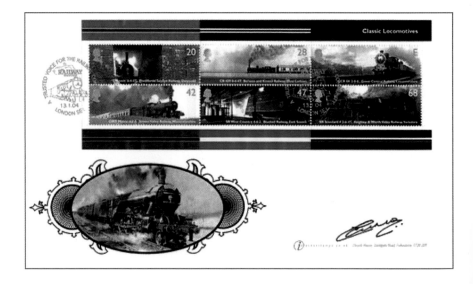

The Railway Magazine also issued a cover for the Age of Steam in 2004 signed by Sir William McAlpine..The second cover was issued for the issue of the Steam Locomotives miniature sheet and is signed by Bob Crow general secretary of the RMT. National Union Rail, Maritime and Transport workers.

A smiler sheet was issued to celebrate the 75th Anniversary of the World Steam Record of 100 mph. The sheet carried the official National Railway Museum, Flying Scotsman logo.

The Anniversary of 200 years of steam was celebrated by a special numbered edition coin cover. The cover carried by 4472 and contains an encapsulated Five pound coin bearing an image of Flying Scotsman inJanuary 2004. The second cover is also a coin cover and uses images of Flying Scotsman on both the cover and coin on the First day cover of the Celebrating Scotland miniature sheet in 2006.

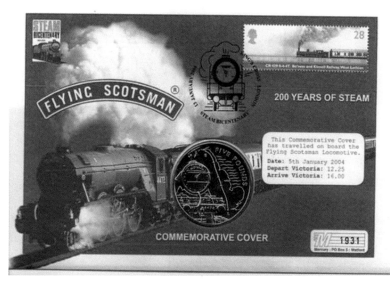

The cover below was for a page from the Inventions Prestige booklet and as well as bearing an image of Flying Scotsman , is signed by Sir William McAlpine.

The next cover is a 75th anniversary coin cover for Flying Scotsman with a 75 year old penny encapsulated and also signed by Sir William McAlpine.

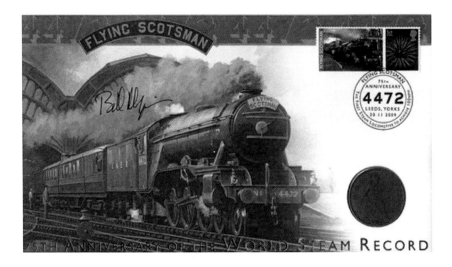

Flying Scotsman is also pictured on a cover celebrating the 60th anniversary of the end of the Big Four particularly the LNER and the formation of British Railways.

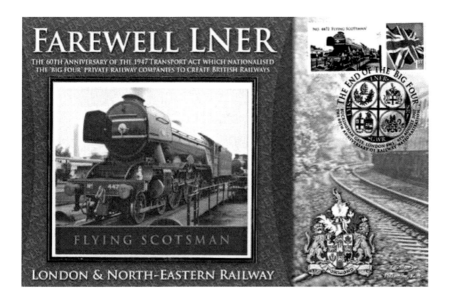

Finally in this section of anniversaries and first day covers using an image if 4472 we have a limited edition cover one of 3000 in the series of Great British Steam engines that was the first day cover of the Classic Locomotives of Scotland.

RETURN TO STEAM 2016.

After a wait of almost ten years the first sight of Flying Scotsman many enthusiasts had was during the locomotives running in on the East Lancs Railway. The photograph of my first sight is reproduced below along with a cover postmarked in Bury to record the preview on 8.Jan 2016.

A Smiler souvenir sheet was produced to celebrate the Return to steam of Flying Scotsman.

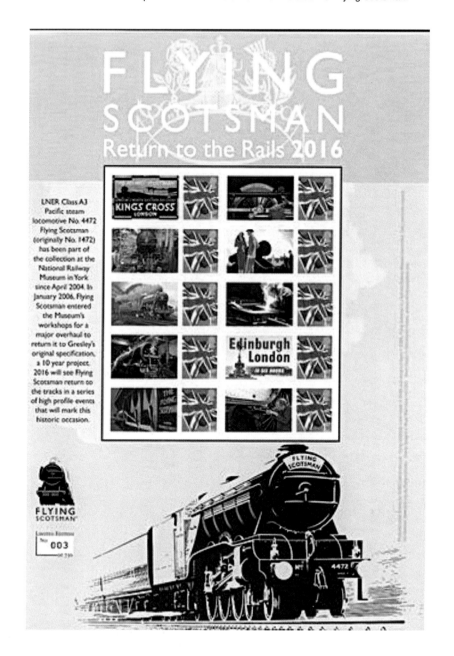

The cover below is an alternative issued by another company for the preview in Bury. The covers use stamps from the Smiler sheet.

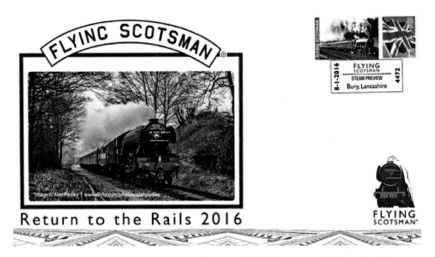

The first mainline run was due on the 23rd of January had to be postponed due to breaking problems. The run was rescheduled for 6-3 2016 from Carnforth to Carlisle. The cover below has postmarks for both proposed and rescheduled runs.

The cover below however only records the postponed run but is decorated with a reproduction of one of the most famous pictures of 4472.

The first scheduled mainline run on 25-Feb-2016 from Kings Cross to York is celebrated by the cover below

This cover by another producer celebrates the inaugural run and was carried on board, this is recorded with a cachet alongside the official Flying Scotsman cachet. The locomotive pictured is not however 60103 but 60135 Madge Wildfire a locomotive that was used to haul the Flying Scotsman the train I.e. "The Journey".

The next cover features the the anniversary of the designer of the A3's Sir Nigel Gresley and carries the same A3 postmark with a date of 5 April 2016, the anniversary of his death when a statue was erected at Kings Cross Station.

This cover was also carried on board, and it can be seen that it is part of a " Return to the rails 2016" series of covers marking each of the events that involved Flying Scotsman in 2016.the second cover was a souvenir of the locomotive's presentation at the National Railway Museum.

The covers from the same series are souvenirs of Flying Scotsman's visit to Scotland, bearing stamps from the smiler sheet, and special postmarks and cachets.

The final covers relate to the last of the National Railway Museums Season of events to welcome 4472/ 60103, back to the rails and was the:-

FLYING SCOTSMAN AND THE SHILDON SHED BASH
Held from July 23, 2016 - July 31, 2016

Inspired by famous "Shed Bashes" of the 1950s and 1960s, when enthusiasts visited a shed and tried to "bag" as many locomotives as possible. Therefore Flying Scotsman was joined by some special guests for this event at Locomotion.

Flying Scotsman was joined by :-

A4 60009 'Union of South Africa'. Q6 63395; V2 4771 'Green Arrow' D9002 Kings Own Yorkshire Light Infantry. Three of which are pictured on the second cover.

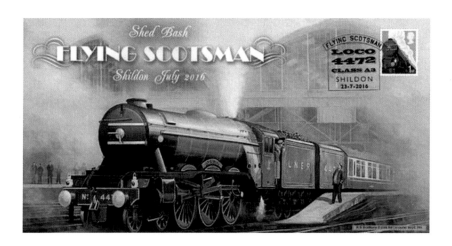

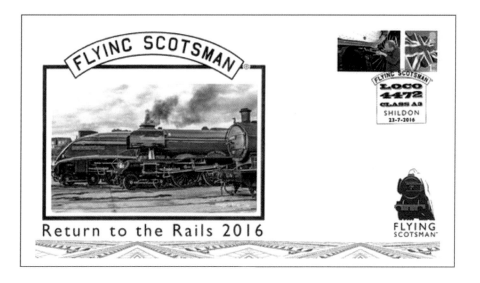

BIBLIOGRAPHY.And suggested further reading :-

Flying Scotsman by Alan Pegler, Cecil J. Allen, Trevor Bailey. Published by Ian Allen 1969

ISBN 7110-0107-3

Railroading magazine Number 33 April 1970. Article on USA tour written at the time.

Flying Scotsman On Tour Australia written by John Dudley. Published by Chapmans 1990

ISBN 1-85592-504-4

The Worlds most famous Steam Locomotive published by Finial and Flying Scotsman Association

1997. 1-900467-02-X

Flying Scotsman, the worlds most Travelled Steam Locomotive by Peter Nicholson published by

Ian Allen 1999. ISBN 0-7110-2744-7

Flying Scotsman the people's engine by Geoffrey Hughes published by Friends of National

Railway Museum Enterprises Ltd. 2005 ISBN 0-9546685-3-7

Flying Scotsman, The Legend Lives On. By Brian Sharpe. Published by Mortons Media Ltd 2009

ISBN 10: 1-845630-90-4

Flying Scotsman the extraordinary story of the world's most famous train by Andrew Roden.

Published by Aurum Press 2007. ISBN-10: 1 84513 2416

Flying Scotsman, the train, the locomotive, the legend, by Bob Gwyne published by Shire

Publications in association with the NRM.2010. ISBM 978-0-74780-770-4

The Flying Scotsman pocket book. Compiled by R.H.N.Hardy Porthouse Publishing, for Conway

books 2013. ISBN 978-84486-222-1

Flying Scotsman the world's most famous steam locomotive.by James S. Baldwin published by Go

Entertainment Group Ltd. 2011 ISBN 5 055298091846

Flying Scotsman.A Legend Reborn by Brian Sharpe. Mortons Media Group 2016 ISBN

978-1909128-84-2

Collect Railways on Stamps. 3rd edition. Stanley Gibbons catalogue. 1999. ISBN 0-85259-436-4.

Flying Scotsman The official Journal of the Flying Scotsman Association 11 issues from 1996

onwards.